Copyright © 2024 Amber T. Ngo

All rights reserved. No part of this book may be reproduced, stored in a retrieval system, or transmitted in any form or by any means, electronic, mechanical, photocopying, recording, or otherwise, without the prior written permission of the copyright owner.

Disclaimer: The information contained in this book is for general informational purposes only. While every effort has been made to ensure the accuracy of the content, the author and publisher assume no responsibility for errors or omissions. The reader is encouraged to verify any information before making travel plans or decisions. Travel conditions and regulations may change; it is advisable to check with relevant authorities and cruise lines.

Table of Contents

Chapter 1: Introduction to Hiking in Norway   7

    1.1 Why Hike in Norway?   7

    1.2 What is New in 2025: Updated Trails and Regulations   9

    1.3 Right to Roam (Allemannsretten): Freedom and Responsibility   11

    1.4 How to Use this Guide.   12

Chapter 2: Preparing for Your Hike   15

2.1 Best Time for Hiking in Norway   15

    2.2 Essential Gear and Packing List   18

    2.3 Safety and Emergency Preparedness   21

    2.4 Understanding Norway's Hiking Difficulty Ratings.   23

    2.5 Trail Navigation using Maps, GPS, and Trail Markers   27

    2.6 Eco-Friendly Hiking: Leave No Trace, Sustainability   28

Chapter 3: Norway's Iconic Hiking Destinations   31

    3.1 Trolltunga, the Legendary Cliff Above the Fjord   31

    3.2 Preikestolen (Pulpit Rock): The Most Popular Viewpoint   33

    3.3 Kjeragbolten, The Boulder Between Two Cliffs   36

3.4 Romsdalseggen Ridge is Norway's most scenic hike. 38

3.5 Besseggen Ridge, The Classic Norwegian Adventure 40

3.6 Hardangervidda National Park is a Vast Wilderness. 42

3.7 Jotunheimen National Park, the Land of Giants 44

Chapter 4: Hidden Gems and Secret Trails. 46

4.1 Lofoten Islands: Hiking With a View of the Sea 46

4.2 Senja's Wild Coast: Norway's Little-Known Hiking Paradise. 49

4.3 Ånderdalen National Park: A Secluded Arctic Escape. 51

Chapter 5: Multi-Day Treks and Long-Distance Hiking Routes. 54

5.1 The King's Trail (Kongevegen over Filefjell): A Historical Journey 55

5.2 The Nordkalottleden Trail, the Arctic Wilderness Route 57

5.3 The Jotunheimen Traverse, The Ultimate Norwegian Challenge 59

Chapter 6: Seasonal Hiking and Unique Experiences. 62

6.1 Midnight Sun Hiking: Trekking Under 24-Hour Daylight 62

6.2 Winter Hiking and Snowshoe Adventures   64

6.3 Top Fall Foliage Hikes in Norway   66

6.4 Seeing the Northern Lights on the Trail.   68

Chapter 7: Practical Information for Hikers.   **70**

7.1 Getting to Trailheads: Transportation and Logistics   70

7.2 Where to Stay: Cabins, Camping, and Hotels.   73

7.3 Hiking with Kids and Families   76

Chapter 8: Local Culture and Hiking Stories   **78**

8.1 Norwegian Folktales and Legends Regarding Mountains   78

8.2 Cultural Hiking Experience with the Sámi People.   81

Chapter 9: Final Tips and Resources.   **84**

9.1 Recommended Hiking Apps and Websites   84

9.2 Emergency Contacts and Resources.   87

9.3 Maps   88

Chapter 1: Introduction to Hiking in Norway

1.1 Why Hike in Norway?

Stepping onto a Norwegian path reminds you why hiking is more than simply exercise—it's a transformative experience. The air is cool, the aroma of pine and wet soil fills your breath, and waterfalls cascade down mountain slopes like silver threads. Norway is more than simply a hiking destination; it is a place to interact with nature in its purest form.

Norway's scenery is a breathtaking combination of spectacular fjords, glacier-carved valleys, and towering peaks that seem to rise directly from the sea. Few nations in the world provide such a wide range of hiking opportunities in one location. You may be standing on the windswept plateau of Hardangervidda, home to wild reindeer, or traveling down the knife-edge ridge of Besseggen, flanked by emerald and sapphire lakes.

Then there are Lofoten's rugged peaks, which rise above white-sand beaches like something out of a dream.

What makes Norway even more unique is its accessibility to the outdoors. You may freely explore huge areas thanks to the country's "Right to Roam" statute (which we will discuss shortly). Well-marked routes, charming mountain lodges (DNT huts), and a strong public transit system make even the most inaccessible regions accessible.

But trekking here is more than simply pursuing spectacular sights. It's about discovering a nation where nature is strongly ingrained in the culture. Norwegians grow up hiking—they even have a name, "friluftsliv," which translates to "open-air life." It's a philosophy that promotes going outside, disconnecting from the contemporary world, and embracing nature's raw beauty.

If you're new to hiking in Norway, this book will teach you all you need to know, from planning and preparation to discovering hidden treasures that most visitors overlook. Whether you're searching for hard multi-day hikes, short picturesque walks, or off-the-beaten-path activities, you'll have an amazing experience.

1.2 What is New in 2025: Updated Trails and Regulations

Norway is continually growing when it comes to sustainable hiking and route building, and 2025 promises interesting changes for both novice and expert hikers.

New and Improved Trails

Several popular roads have been upgraded this year:
- **Trolltunga Alternative Route:** To relieve congestion on the main route, a new additional path has been created, complete with enhanced guidance and breathtaking new views.
- **Lofoten's Mountain Paths:** To safeguard the delicate Arctic habitat, some routes now have new wooden decks and erosion control measures due to increasing foot traffic.
- **Senja's Wild Coast Expansion:** New trail connections allow you to trek between prominent coastline overlooks without retracing your steps.

Accessibility Enhancements

Norway makes hiking more inclusive:
- Improved signage with multilingual information is now accessible on popular routes.
- Trail grading upgrades provide hikers with a better understanding of what to anticipate before they start.
- More public transit alternatives now connect major trailheads with adjacent towns, eliminating the need for rental automobiles.

Regulation Updates for Sustainable Hiking.

With a rising number of hikers each year, Norway has implemented new criteria.
- **Camping Restrictions:** Some high-traffic sites now demand camping permits to reduce environmental effects.
- **Drone Regulations:** More trails have been marked as drone-free zones to protect animals and the natural experience.
- **Wildlife Protection:** To preserve musk oxen and reindeer populations, several roads in Dovrefjell and Jotunheimen are currently limited during calving season.

These upgrades guarantee that Norway remains one of the world's most stunning and well-preserved hiking destinations—and this book will help you easily negotiate these changes.

1.3 Right to Roam (Allemannsretten): Freedom and Responsibility

In Norway, nature belongs to everyone. You can explore woods, mountains, and beaches thanks to the country's Right to Roam statute, or "Allemannsretten"—even on privately held territory.

What does this mean for you?

- You may walk, camp, and visit most natural places without requiring special authorization.
- You may camp anywhere for free, as long as it is at least 150 meters from the next home or cabin.
- You have access to freshwater lakes and streams, ideal for filling your bottle with crisp, glacier-fed water.

Your Responsibility as a Hiker

With this independence comes the responsibility to safeguard Norway's environment:

■ Respect private property: Follow designated paths while crossing through agricultural or private land.

■ Leave No Trace: Remove litter, do not pick wildflowers, and avoid upsetting animals.

■ Follow Campfire Rules: Open fires are forbidden in wooded areas from April 15 to September 15 due to wildfire danger.

■ Respect Local Communities: While small mountain towns welcome hikers, it's important to respect their land and culture.

This legislation is one of Norway's most valuable gifts to outdoor enthusiasts, and when followed, it assures that the environment stays clean for future generations.

1.4 How to Use this Guide.

This book is intended to be your hiking companion, whether you are a first-time tourist or an experienced adventurer. Here's how to make the most of it.

Understanding Trail Ratings

Hikes in Norway are classified by difficulty level, allowing you to pick the ideal experience.

● Easy: Short, well-marked paths with little elevation rise (e.g., Vøringsfossen Waterfall Walk).

● Moderate: Longer paths with uneven terrain and moderate climbs (e.g., Preikestolen).

● Difficulty: steep ascents, lengthy distances, or exposure to high altitude conditions (e.g., Romsdalseggen Ridge).

● Expert - Technical hikes include climbing, glacier crossings, or overnight treks (e.g., Stetind, Norway's "Matterhorn").

Navigation and Wayfinding

- This book has extensive route descriptions, GPS information, and elevation maps.
- Maps and applications: We propose the finest hiking maps and smartphone applications for real-time navigation.
- Alternative Routes: For several routes, we've included less-crowded alternatives that provide comparable vistas with fewer people.

What You Can Find in Each Chapter

- Chapter 2 provides packing lists, safety instructions, and seasonal suggestions.
- Chapters 3-5 explore Norway's most magnificent treks, ranging from well-known paths to undiscovered treasures.
- Chapter 6 delves into uncommon seasonal activities, such as trekking beneath the Midnight Sun or chasing the Northern Lights.
- Chapter 7 discusses practical topics such as transportation, lodging, and local culture.

Norway welcomes you to experience its glaciers, fjords, and summits. Whether you're going on a bucket-list trek like Trolltunga or looking for a quiet path where you won't see another human, this guide will ensure you're completely equipped and motivated. So, tie up your boots, pack your bag, and let's begin your Norwegian adventure!

Chapter 2: Preparing for Your Hike

2.1 Best Time for Hiking in Norway

Norway's landscapes change greatly throughout the year, so picking the ideal time to walk may make or break your journey.

I will never forget my first trek in Norway. It was early May, and I was excited to tackle the trails. I laced my boots, packed my backpack with refreshments, and headed off for Trolltunga, one of the country's most renowned vistas. But halfway up the slope, reality struck me: heavy snow, an unmarked path, and no one else in sight. It was lovely, but also chilly, slippery, and considerably more perilous than I had anticipated. Lesson learned: time is essential while trekking in Norway.

Let's talk about when you should and shouldn't go trekking.

Spring (March-May): Proceed with Caution.
- The days are getting longer, but high-altitude paths remain blanketed in snow and ice.
- Lower-elevation walks (coastal regions and woodland paths) begin to open up, but mountain routes may be risky.

April and May are unpredictable—
- One day it's bright and pleasant, and the next it's snowing.
- Ideal for coastal treks, lower valleys, and fjord trips.

Summer (June - August): Peak hiking season.
- The ideal time to hike in Norway! Snow melts, paths reopen, and the landscapes are at their greenest.
- The Midnight Sun (north of the Arctic Circle) implies 24 hours of daylight, so you may trek at 2 a.m. if you wish!
- Most mountain accommodations (DNT huts) and ferries are at maximum capacity.
- Downsides? Popular paths such as Preikestolen and Trolltunga get busy.

- Ideal for: fjord treks, glacier walks, mountain peaks, and long-distance hiking.

Autumn (September–October): Stunning Colors, Fewer Crowds

- September is one of the greatest months for trekking due to fewer people, milder temperatures, and the golden fall hues.
- Snow begins to return to the mountains in mid-October.
- If you prefer calm trails without the summer throng, early October is ideal.
- Ideal for mountain climbs, fjord routes, and off-the-beaten-path experiences.

Winter (November–February): Only for the Brave

- Most routes are covered in thick snow, making regular trekking impossible.
- Ski touring and snowshoeing have replaced conventional hiking.
- Polar Night (north of the Arctic Circle) implies less daylight in December and January.
- Best for: Northern Lights treks (guided), snowshoe excursions, and ski trekking.

When to Avoid Hiking?

✘ Early spring (March-April): High avalanche danger and muddy routes due to melting snow.

✘ Late autumn (November): Trails freeze as sunshine hours decrease.

✘ Anytime during severe weather warnings.

⧖ Quick answer? July, August, and September are your safest bets.

2.2 Essential Gear and Packing List

There is a Norwegian saying:

"Det finnes ikke dårlig vaer, bare dårlige klær."

Translation? "There's no such thing as bad weather, only bad clothing."

Hiking in Norway requires being prepared for everything—rain, wind, sun, and even snow, sometimes all on the same day. A brilliant blue sky may transform into dense fog in minutes, and if you're not properly equipped, it can quickly transition from adventure to survival.

Here's what you should carry for a successful Norwegian walk.

Clothing: Layer Like a Pro.

■ Base Layer (Moisture-Wicking): Merino wool or synthetic fabric (not cotton!)

■ Mid-layer insulation: Fleece or lightweight down jacket.

■ Outer layer (waterproof/windproof): Gore-Tex or equivalent shell jacket

■ Pants: Hiking trousers (avoid jeans since they become chilly and wet quickly).

■ Bring a hat and gloves since the Norwegian highlands may be chilly even during the summer.

■ Wool socks provide dry and happy feet.

💡 Pro tip: Always bring a rain jacket. Norway's weather is unpredictable, even in the summer.

Footwear: The Right Boots Matter.

■ Hiking Boots (Waterproof, High-Ankle Support): Perfect for tough terrain.

■ Trail Runners (Only for Easy Fjord Trails): Ideal for light walks, not suitable for mountains.

■ Gaiters (optional): Keep snow and muck out of boots.

Gear and Essentials

🎒 Backpack (20-30L for day hikes; 50L+ for multi-day trips)

💧 Water Bottle (1.5L+): Most Norwegian streams are safe to drink from.

🍫 Snacks (energy bars, almonds, chocolate): No convenience shops in the highlands!

🗺 Map and compass (or GPS app like UT.no)

🔦 Headlamp (with extra batteries) - Ideal for fall and winter.

🩹 First Aid Kit including blister care, medicines, and bandages.

🚀 Emergency Bivy or Space Blanket—Just in case

⬛ Optional extras
- Trekking poles: Saves your knees on steep descents
- Bug Spray: If trekking near water in the summer.
- Sunscreen and sunglasses: Required for high-altitude or glacier excursions.

2.3 Safety and Emergency Preparedness

Let's be honest: Norway's mountains are stunning, but they don't care about your plans. Weather changes quickly, terrain may be steep and treacherous, and mobile service is often unavailable. Being prepared is not just wise; it might save your life.

Learn the "Mountain Code" (Fjellvettreglene).

Norwegians observe these nine mountain guidelines to keep safe:

1. Plan your trip and inform a buddy. Use applications such as Varsom Regobs to assess trail conditions.

2. Adapt to weather and conditions by checking Yr.no for updates. If terrible weather approaches, turn back.

3. Be prepared for bad weather and cold - Even in summer, gloves and a hat may be needed.

4. Pack enough food, water, and gear - don't assume there's a hut or store nearby.

5. Use a map and compass instead of GPS applications, which may run out of battery.

6. Know Your Limits - If a path is labeled as "expert," avoid pushing it if you're not confident.

7. Don't Go Alone (If You're Inexperienced): While solo treks are fantastic, they may be risky in isolated locations.

8. Turn Back if Necessary - It's okay to call it a day if the circumstances are risky.

9. Conserve energy and seek shelter if needed. If lost, keep still and wait for assistance.

Emergency Contacts and What to Do If Something Goes Wrong.

- Call 112 for an emergency rescue. (If there's no signal, try texting.)
- Norwegian Rescue Services (Red Cross and Alpine Rescue Teams) are well-equipped, but only call when essential.
- If you become lost, wear bright attire to make yourself apparent to helicopters.
- Winter hikers should download the Varsom app for avalanche alerts.

2.4 Understanding Norway's Hiking Difficulty Ratings.

Norway's hiking paths vary from easy, family-friendly excursions to difficult, high-altitude scrambles that challenge even the most experienced hikers. Before you go, make sure you understand the trail ratings so you can choose a trek that is appropriate for your fitness level, experience, and comfort with tough terrain.

I once observed a group of tourists start Besseggen Ridge, a well-known but strenuous hike, wearing casual shoes and carrying a single bottle of water. They imagined it would be an easy trek since it was "popular." After a few hours, they were weary, sliding on the rocks, and regretting their choice. Knowing the difficulty levels is important not just for planning, but also for remaining safe.

Norway's Standard Trail Difficulty System

Most trails in Norway follow a color-coded system to indicate difficulty:

Difficulty Level	Color Code	Description	Examples
Easy (Lett)	● Green	Mostly flat or gently sloping. Well-marked trails. Suitable for beginners, families, and those with limited hiking experience.	Preikestolen (Pulpit Rock), Gjevilvatnet Lake Trail

Medium (Middels)	● Blue	Moderate inclines, some rocky or uneven terrain. Requires a basic fitness level.	Besseggen Ridge, Romsdalseggen Ridge
Challenging (Krevende)	● Red	Steep ascents, longer distances, may require some scrambling. Good fitness and proper hiking gear required.	Trolltunga, Segla, Reinebringen (Full Trail)

| Expert (Ekspert) | ● Black | Very steep, often exposed trails with potential rock climbing sections. Suitable only for experienced hikers with proper gear. | Skåla Summit, Stetind, Innerdalen Peak |

💡 Tip: If you're new to hiking in Norway, start with a green or blue path before progressing to red or black-rated excursions.

2.5 Trail Navigation using Maps, GPS, and Trail Markers

Although Norwegian trails are well-marked, navigating might be difficult in rural regions or during inclement weather. Many hikers believe their phone's GPS will be sufficient—until they lose service halfway up a mountain. Knowing how to navigate correctly is vital.

Trail Markers and What They Mean
- Red "T" Marks ■ are the most popular markings, painted on rocks or trees. Located on all approved Norwegian Trekking Association (DNT) paths.
- Cairns (Stone Piles) ▲ - Used in rocky regions when paint does not cling. Always follow the next conspicuous cairn.
- Wooden signposts ⚑ at trailheads and important crossroads provide distances and anticipated trekking times.
- Blue and white markers ●○ indicate winter paths. These routes often change from summer trails owing to snow conditions.

⚑ Pro tip: If you lose the path, stop and retrace your steps to the previous marker. Don't keep going blindly.

Best Navigational Tools for Hiking in Norway

■ UT.no (App & Website) is Norway's top hiking app, with comprehensive maps, GPS tracking, and route descriptions.

■ Norgeskart (Norwegian Mapping Authority) provides excellent topographic maps.

■ Paper maps and compass are essential for multi-day treks in locations without cell coverage.

■ Use offline GPS apps like Gaia GPS, Maps.me, or AllTrails to download maps before hiking in the mountains.

▲ Safety Tip: Always have a backup navigation technique. Batteries expire, signals fail, and the weather may make vision difficult.

2.6 Eco-Friendly Hiking: Leave No Trace, Sustainability

Norway's natural beauty is pure for a reason: the government prioritizes environmental protection, and hikers must do the same. The "Right to Roam" (Allemannsretten) allows everyone access to nature, but with that freedom comes responsibility.

I recall trekking near Kjeragbolten, a beautiful boulder trapped between rocks. As I approached the peak, I saw something unexpected: a mound of rubbish beside the route. It was distressing to see such a beautiful area abused so carelessly. Norway's wilderness relies on us to keep it pristine.

How to Hike Responsibly in Norway

■ Pack out all trash since there are no rubbish containers on trails. Carry everything with you.

■ Follow marked trails and avoid trampling vulnerable plants. Moss, lichen, and wildflowers take years to regrow.

■ Respect wildlife - Maintain a safe distance from animals, particularly reindeer, and birds during the breeding season.

■ Use eco-friendly toiletries like biodegradable soap and wipes. No toilet paper was left behind!

■ Norway has severe fire rules, therefore no campfires above the treeline. Use a camp stove instead.

Norway's Conservation Efforts

- National Parks and Protected Areas - Over 40 national parks guarantee that nature remains wild.

- Sustainable Trail Maintenance: To avoid erosion, several pathways are fortified with stone stairs and boardwalks.
- Tourism Impact Management - To safeguard vulnerable environments, popular treks like Trolltunga now have guest limitations and need mandated shuttle services.

💡 Want to give back? Join a DNT volunteer program to help maintain the trails!

Hiking in Norway is about more than simply breathtaking vistas; it's also about respecting the land, navigating sensibly, and selecting paths that are appropriate for your skill level. Following these recommendations will ensure that you have a memorable journey while also preserving Norway's nature for future hikers.

Now, let's explore Norway's most magnificent walks, from well-known fjords to secret treasures only locals know about! 🔺✨

Chapter 3: Norway's Iconic Hiking Destinations

3.1 Trolltunga, the Legendary Cliff Above the Fjord

I believed I was prepared for my first trek up Trolltunga. I had read all of the blogs, packed my kit, and was eager to visit the famed tongue-shaped rock hanging 700 meters over Ringedalsvatnet Lake. But about midway through the 27-kilometer round journey, when the wind kicked up and the route became a seemingly unending incline, I realized I had miscalculated the trek.

Trolltunga is not for the faint at heart. It's one of Norway's most difficult but rewarding walks, with breathtaking views of fjords, mountains, and glaciers. If you want to tackle this famed path, here's everything you need to know to do it safely and enjoyably.

Hike Overview

- Distance: 27 kilometers (round trip).
- Duration: 10–12 hours
- Elevation Gain: Approximately 1,200 meters.
- Difficulty: Challenging (Red - Demanding).
- Season: Mid-June to September (ideal period)

What to expect on the trail.

- The First Climb: The first 1 km is quite steep. You'll ascend around 400 meters straight immediately.
- Rolling Terrain: After a rough start, the track flattens out but varies between rocky roads, wooden planks, and swampy sections.
- The Final Stretch: The final five kilometers are lengthy, but once you see Trolltunga, you'll forget about your hurting legs.

Insider Tips for the Best Experience.

■ Arrive on the path around 6 a.m. to avoid crowds and enjoy optimal lighting.

■ Avoid the peak summer rush - July and early August are busy. Visit around mid-September for a more tranquil experience.

■ Be Weather-Ready: The weather may change quickly. Bring waterproof layers and warm clothes, even in the heat.

■ Stay Overnight (Optional): Camping near Trolltunga offers dawn views without crowds.

Safety Tips

■ Avoid Hiking in Bad Weather - If rain or fog is expected, postpone your trip. Wet rocks equal perilous situations.

■ Bring a headlamp - If you take longer than intended, you'll need illumination for the return trip.

■ Know Your Limits - This is a long and tough journey. If you're not accustomed to hiking full-day hikes, choose a shorter option like Reinebringen.

3.2 Preikestolen (Pulpit Rock): The Most Popular Viewpoint

Some treks are notable due to their difficulty. Others are notable for being both strikingly gorgeous and easily accessible. Preikestolen (Pulpit Rock) comes into the second category, which explains why it is one of Norway's most popular treks.

I recall reaching the summit on a fresh summer morning, just as the first rays of sunshine lit the 604-meter-high rock jutting out over Lysefjorden. The quiet was broken only by gasps of wonder as trekkers took in the scenery—it seemed like they were on the end of the planet.

Hike Overview
- Distance: 8 kilometers (round trip).
- Duration: 4–5 hours
- Elevation gain: around 500 meters.
- Difficulty: Moderate (Blue - Suitable for most hikers).
- Season: April-October (ideal time)

What to expect on the trail.
- Gradual Ascent: The path has some steep portions, but Nepalese Sherpas erected stone stairs to make it easier.
- Scenic Rest Stops: Several plateaus along the journey provide breathtaking views—ideal for a stop and some photographs.

- The Last Approach: The last stretch is on an exposed rocky terrain, leading to the iconic flat cliff.

When is the best time to visit for an unforgettable experience?

■ Hike at sunrise or sunset to avoid daytime crowds. Sunrise treks provide wonderful illumination.

■ Shoulder Seasons (April-May & September-October): Fewer visitors, milder temps, and as spectacular.

■ Winter (For the Brave): Guided walks provide a unique snow-covered experience.

Photography Tips

■ Take a wide-angle lens to catch the whole drop-off and fjord.

■ Golden Hour Magic - The most spectacular lighting occurs at sunset and dawn.

■ Due to severe drone limitations, you'll need to use handheld photography instead.

Safety Tips

🔔 Stay away from the edge! - There are no rails, and severe winds are unexpected.

🔔 Beware of Wet Rocks - If it has rained lately, the final rock surface might be slippery.

🔔 Don't underestimate the descent. Many hikers feel wonderful at the top but suffer on the way down. Take your time.

3.3 Kjeragbolten, The Boulder Between Two Cliffs

Kjeragbolten is one walk in Norway that makes even the boldest hikers question their decisions. Why? Because it concludes with you standing on a rock trapped between two cliffs, with a 984-meter plunge underneath you.

I recall the first time I stepped atop the boulder. My pulse was pounding, my palms were sweaty, and my mind was screaming, "One wrong step and you're done!" But as soon as I placed my feet and gazed out over Lysefjorden, the terror converted to pure joy.

Hike Overview
- Distance: 11 kilometers (round trip).
- Duration: 6–8 hours
- Elevation gain: around 800 meters.
- Difficulty: Challenging (Red - Demanding).
- Season: June-September (ideal time)

What to expect on the trail.
- Steep Climbs with Chains: You'll climb numerous steep parts with metal chains fastened in the rock.
- Rocky and exposed terrain: The track is largely bare rock, however, some exposed spots demand cautious footing.
- The Boulder Itself: To stand atop Kjeragbolten, you must cautiously walk onto the rock, which is bigger than it seems yet still intimidating.

How to Take the Best Kjeragbolten Photo
🎒 Having confidence is essential, since hesitation may make things more difficult. Step gently onto the boulder.
🎒 Use a wide-angle lens to capture the spectacular drop behind you.

🪧 Consider having someone else take your photo - taking selfies might be unsafe. Find another hiker and capture your moment.

Safety Tips

🪧 Only attempt in dry weather since the rock becomes very slippery when wet.

🪧 Wear Good Hiking Shoes - You'll need strong boots with great grip.

🪧 Know Your Limits - You don't need to walk on the boulder to enjoy the view. Many individuals just watch and snap photographs.

3.4 Romsdalseggen Ridge is Norway's most scenic hike.

When I initially arrived at Romsdalseggen, I had no idea what to anticipate. I'd heard rumors about its beauty—that it was dubbed Norway's most spectacular ridge hike—but nothing could have prepared me for the sheer magnificence of the environment. Standing on the crest, I felt as if I were soaring above the globe, with the emerald-green Rauma River winding below, rugged peaks piercing the sky, and distant fjords gleaming in the sunlight.

Hike Overview
- Distance: 10 kilometers (point-to-point).
- Duration: 6–8 hours
- Elevation Gain: Approximately 970 meters
- Difficulty: Challenging (Red - Demanding).
- Season: July-September (ideal time)

What makes Romsdalseggen unique?

■ A small slope offers breathtaking panoramic views of fjords, valleys, and majestic peaks.

■ Wild & Untamed Beauty - Romsdalseggen, unlike other popular treks, has a raw, untouched vibe.

The trek offers one of the greatest views of Europe's biggest vertical rock wall, Trollveggen (Troll Wall).

What to expect on the trail.
- A Tough Start: The first three kilometers are hard and unrelenting, ascending about 800 meters.
- The slope Walk: Once at the top, the narrow slope provides stunning views in all directions.
- Trekking poles are recommended for the lengthy, knee-testing descent into Åndalsnes.

Insider Tips for an Epic Experience.

■ Start Early to Beat the Crowds - As this walk becomes increasingly popular, an early start ensures a calmer ridge.

■ Take the Romsdalseggen Bus: The path is one-way, so take the morning shuttle from Åndalsnes to the trailhead.

■ Dress in layers since the ridge may be windy and unpredictable.

3.5 Besseggen Ridge, The Classic Norwegian Adventure

Besseggen Ridge is a walk that everyone in Norway is familiar with. This track is strongly ingrained in Norwegian hiking culture, and with good reason: where else can you walk on a knife-edge ridge with a deep blue fjord on one side and a turquoise glacier-fed lake on the other?

I will never forget my first time crossing the ridge. As I ascended the steep portion leading to the summit, I saw hikers ahead of me pausing to take in the vista, their breath taken away not just by the exertion, but also by the pure beauty of the scenery.

Hike Overview
- Distance: 14 kilometers (point-to-point).
- Duration: 6–8 hours
- Elevation Gain: Approximately 1,200 meters.
- Difficulty: Challenging (Red - Demanding).
- Season: June-September (ideal time)

Why hike Besseggen?

■ Norway's Most Famous Ridge Walk - A must-do walk for both residents and visitors.

■ Witness the stunning contrast between Gjende (turquoise lake) and Bessvatnet (deep blue lake).

■ National Pride: Besseggen is a popular route in Norway, with around 60,000 hikers annually.

What to expect on the trail.
- Boat or Hike First? Most hikers take the boat from Gjendesheim to Memurubu and then trek back.
- The Iconic Ridge Climb: The most difficult section of the trip is the scramble up the narrow Besseggen Ridge, which necessitates hands-on climbing at times.

- The Final Stretch: Following the crest, the route slowly descends to Gjendesheim, offering breathtaking vistas along the way.

Pro Tips for a Smooth Hike.

■ Book the Boat in Advance: The boat from Gjendesheim to Memurubu sells out swiftly during high season.

■ Prepare for Steep Climbs: The ridge demands scrambling over rocks, so fitness is essential.

■ Visit on a Clear Day: Cloudy weather might conceal the breathtaking lake contrast that makes this climb renowned.

3.6 Hardangervidda National Park is a Vast Wilderness.

If you've ever wanted to go in a huge, unspoiled wilderness where reindeer graze freely and paths extend for days, Hardangervidda is the place to go. This high-altitude plateau is Norway's biggest national park, with many hiking options ranging from short day walks to multi-day expeditions.

Why hike in Hardangervidda?
■ Northern Europe's largest mountain plateau offers expansive views.
■ Wildlife Encounters - Visit one of Europe's few remaining wild reindeer habitats.
■ Suitable for Multi-Day Treks - With many hiking cabins and defined paths, it's great for longer excursions.

Best Hiking Routes.
- Hårteigen Summit (1,691m) is a tough but rewarding summit with great panoramic views.
- The Wild Reindeer Route is a multi-day hike over old reindeer migratory routes.
- Haukeliseter to Finse is a typical hut-to-hut journey in the center of the park.

Professional Tips for Exploring Hardangervidda
■ Pack for All Weather - Even in summer, temperatures may fall below freezing at night.
■ Use DNT Cabins - Norway's Tourist Association huts provide great accommodations for multi-day hikes.
■ Respect wildlife - Maintain a safe distance from reindeer herds and respect Leave No Trace principles.

3.7 Jotunheimen National Park, the Land of Giants

If you wish to trek amid Norway's tallest peaks, Jotunheimen is the perfect place. With towering mountains, glacier-fed lakes, and some of Norway's most famous paths, this park is a must-see for experienced hikers.

My first journey in Jotunheimen took me to the peak of Galdhøpiggen, Northern Europe's tallest mountain, and I felt like I was on top of the world. The air was thin, the scenery was unearthly, and the feeling of achievement was unparalleled.

Why hike in Jotunheimen?

■ Home to Norway's tallest peaks, including Galdhøpiggen (2,469m) and Glittertind (2,464m).

■ Trails are challenging and rewarding, ranging from simple valley treks to demanding mountain ascents.

■ Glacier Adventures - Some walks feature glacier crossings that need a guide and specific equipment.

Top Hiking Routes in Jotunheimen
- Galdhøpiggen (Norway's Highest Peak) is a 6- to 8-hour climb to the summit of Scandinavia.
- Glittertind (Almost as High as Galdhøpiggen!) is a somewhat easier but equally picturesque mountain.
- The Jotunheimen Traverse is a strenuous multi-day journey connecting numerous peaks.

Professional Tips for Hiking in Jotunheimen
■ Be prepared for snow - Even in July, certain routes may still have snowfields to navigate.

■ Consider a Guide for Glacier Hikes: Some paths need ropes and ice axes.

■ Train for Elevation Gain - These treks need high fitness due to the steep climbs.

Whether you're climbing a renowned ridge like Besseggen, exploring the wilderness of Hardangervidda, or conquering the gigantic peaks of Jotunheimen, Norway's landscapes will steal your breath away—in every meaning of the term.

Chapter 4: Hidden Gems and Secret Trails.

Sometimes the finest treks in Norway aren't the ones you see on Instagram. While Trolltunga, Preikestolen, and Besseggen attract thousands of hikers each year, there are still spots where you may walk for hours without seeing another soul—places where the scenery seems pristine and every bend in the route delivers something surprising.

This chapter is for you if you desire seclusion, spectacular vistas without crowds, and a genuine feeling of adventure. Let's discover Norway's best-kept hiking secrets—trails that provide everything from spectacular coastal cliffs to Arctic wilderness but without the crowds.\

4.1 Lofoten Islands: Hiking With a View of the Sea

I will never forget my first walk in the Lofoten Islands. I was standing on top of Reinebringen, looking down at Reine's little red fishing houses, their reflections glittering in the crystal-clear fjord underneath. Behind me, craggy peaks rose straight from the water, like something out of a fairytale story. It seemed weird, like standing on the edge of the planet.

The Lofoten Islands are home to some of Norway's most stunning landscapes, where mountains meet the sea in ways that defy logic. Hiking here is unlike any place else—the routes are steep, the scenery is breathtaking, and the benefits are immediate and memorable.

Best Hikes in the Lofoten Islands.
Reinebringen (Easy-Moderate): 3 km round trip.
- The Classic Lofoten vista - A steep but short hike to a renowned vista of Reine and the fjords.
- Stone Steps All the Way - Thanks to a recently constructed Sherpa stairway, the trek is now more accessible than previously.
- Go at sunrise or late evening to avoid the throng and enjoy the golden glow of Arctic light.

▲ Ryten and Kvalvika Beach (Moderate): 7 km round trip.
- Panoramic Coastal Views - A picturesque trek to one of Lofoten's most popular beaches.

- Swim in the Arctic? - If you're feeling courageous, swim in the blue waters of Kvalvika Beach.
- Less Crowded Alternative - Provides a comparable experience as Reinebringen but with far fewer people.

▲ Hermannsdalstinden (Difficult): 20 km round trip

- Lofoten's Highest Peak - A tough full-day excursion with panoramic views of the whole archipelago.
- True Wilderness Experience - Few visitors visit here, making it an ideal destination for individuals seeking seclusion.

Insider Tips for Lofoten Hiking

■ Weather may change quickly, so pack clothes and be prepared for sun, rain, and wind in one day.

■ Visit in late summer or early fall for fewer tourists, warmer temps, and an opportunity to see the Northern Lights.

■ Respect the Local Culture: Many paths run past the private property and traditional fishing communities; leaving no trace.

4.2 Senja's Wild Coast: Norway's Little-Known Hiking Paradise.

If Lofoten is the famous sibling, Senja is the more outgoing twin. Located north of Lofoten, this craggy island provides similarly breathtaking vistas but with a fraction of the visitors. Sheer cliffs tumble into the sea, isolated coves lie behind towering peaks, and the trails are among Norway's best-kept secrets.

I initially went to Senja on a whim, pulled in by reports of breathtaking vistas without the throng. I ended up ascending Segla, a jagged mountain crest that rises like a blade from the coast. Standing on the peak, with nothing but sea and sky extending out in every direction, I felt I had discovered something extraordinary.

Best Hikes in Senja.

▲ **Segla (Moderate-Difficult): 5 km round trip**
- Senja's Most Famous View - A tough, rewarding climb to a jagged mountain perched over the fjord.
- The best time to see the Golden Arctic Light painting the mountains is around sunrise or sunset.

▲ **Hesten (Moderate): 4 km round trip.**
- The Best Vista of Segla - For the classic postcard vista of Segla proper, trek Hesten instead.
- Easier Alternative - A less challenging hike with equally breathtaking views.

▲ **Husfjellet (Easy-Moderate): 8 km round trip.**
- Sweeping Coastal Views - A modest ascent leads to one of Norway's top sunset sites.
- Perfect for Beginners - Less technical than Segla, but as gorgeous.

Why hike in Senja instead of Lofoten?

■ Senja remains a hidden gem, although Lofoten is well-known.

■ Stunning scenery, including jagged peaks, deep fjords, and beautiful beaches, but with more pristine wilderness.

■ Ideal for Northern Lights Chasers - With less light pollution, Norway offers some of the greatest aurora sightings.

4.3 Ånderdalen National Park: A Secluded Arctic Escape.

Ånderdalen, located deep inside Senja, is one of Norway's least-visited national parks. If you want serenity, pristine Arctic wilderness, and a genuine back-to-nature experience, this is the place to go.

During my trip around Ånderdalen, I scarcely saw anybody else. Instead, I wandered through vast pine woods, across crystal-clear rivers, and saw wild reindeer wandering gently through the mist. It seemed like going back in time to Norway before tourists, people, and highways.

Why hike in Ånderdalen?

■ Unspoiled Arctic wilderness, including woods, marshes, lakes, and mountains.

■ Wildlife Encounters: Home to moose, lynx, eagles, and one of Norway's few wild reindeer herds.

■ Ideal for Multi-Day Treks - Well-marked routes lead to secluded cottages, allowing for hut-to-hut trekking.

Best Trails in Ånderdalen.

▲ Åndervatnet Trail (Easy): 5 km round trip.

A Gentle Introduction to the Park - A pleasant trek through pine trees that leads to a serene lake.

▲ Ånderdalen Circuit (Moderate): 14 km round trip.

A Full-Day Exploration - A picturesque circle via lakes, marshes, and woodland paths.

▲ Difficult multi-day wilderness trek covering 30-50 kilometers.

Go Deep into the Wild - Spend 2-3 days trekking through the park, stopping at secluded DNT cottages along the route.

Tips to Explore Ånderdalen

■ Prepare with a map and compass since certain areas of the park may not have phone coverage.

■ Maintain a safe distance from moose and reindeer and respect the sensitive Arctic ecology.

■ Enjoy the Silence - This is one of Norway's quietest places—enjoy the tranquility.

Not all excursions have to be on the beaten road. If you want to see Norway at its most wild, distant, and stunning, these hidden jewels will shift your perspective on the nation.

In the next chapter, we'll explore Norway's top multi-day hikes—where the real adventures begin!

Chapter 5: Multi-Day Treks and Long-Distance Hiking Routes.

Multi-day hiking has a unique quality—a feeling of freedom, adventure, and a profound connection with nature that a short day trek cannot provide. The sense of waking up in the bush, hearing nothing but the wind and the distant sound of birds, knowing that today's road would take you farther into the unknown—that's what makes long-distance hiking so transforming.

If you've ever wanted to roam over wide plateaus, climb through steep mountain passes, or follow in the footsteps of historic explorers, Norway has some of the world's most stunning multi-day excursions. Whether you're looking for a historic pilgrimage path, an Arctic wilderness journey, or a high-altitude alpine adventure, this chapter will take you through Norway's top long-distance walks and multi-day treks.

5.1 The King's Trail (Kongevegen over Filefjell): A Historical Journey

There's something special about traveling along a route that has been utilized by many travelers for ages. The Kongevegen over Filefjell, also known as The King's Road, is more than simply a hiking route; it's a piece of living history.

This old roadway was initially established in the late 18th century as a royal road between Oslo and Bergen. It was the first true route connecting eastern and western Norway, utilized by merchants, tourists, and even monarchs. Much of the road has been rebuilt and converted into a beautiful hiking trail that winds through mountain valleys, lush woods, and historical landmarks.

Why should you hike the King's Trail?

■ Take a historical journey in Norway, passing by old stone bridges, waystations, and farmhouses.

■ Easy and accessible - This route is modest and well-marked, suitable for both novices and history enthusiasts.

■ Beautiful scenery - Explore the finest of Norwegian nature, from rolling green meadows to towering peaks.

Trail Details:

- Distance: 100 km (may be completed in shorter chunks)
- Time required: 4–6 days
- Difficulty: Easy to Moderate.
- The best time to hike is from June to September.

Accommodations include historic hotels, farm stays, and mountain lodges along the road.

Insider Tips

■ Take Your Time - Enjoy the path gently, stopping at historic sites and chatting with locals.

■ Stay in a Historic Lodge - Enjoy authentic Norwegian hospitality at one of the historic mountain inns.

■ Combine with a picturesque Train Ride: The walk is near the famed Flåm Railway, one of the most picturesque train trips in the world.

5.2 The Nordkalottleden Trail, the Arctic Wilderness Route

If you want a real wilderness trip, far from civilization, where you may go for days without seeing another person, the Nordkalottleden Trail is the ultimate Arctic expedition.

This 800-kilometer trek passes across three countries—Norway, Sweden, and Finland—and takes hikers deep into the untamed Arctic tundra. The scenery is harsh, lonely, and breathtakingly beautiful, with immense tundras, glacier-fed rivers, and wild reindeer herds grazing freely.

I encountered a fellow hiker on this path, who informed me:

"Out here, you're not just walking—you're surviving. You feel the land in a way you never do on shorter hikes."

It is true. This is a path for individuals who want true adventure, don't mind carrying all they need on their backs, and are eager to see the Arctic's raw, untamed beauty.

Why should you hike the Nordkalottleden Trail?

■ Hike across three countries to experience diverse landscapes and cultures.

■ Experience ultimate solitude and wild camping on one of Europe's least frequented long-distance paths.

■ Wildlife Encounters - Look for reindeer, Arctic foxes, and wolverines.

Trail Details:

- Distance: 800 kilometers (may be done in portions).
- Time required: 1-2 months (or shorter chunks of 1-2 weeks).
- Difficulty: Hard (remote terrain and uncertain weather)
- Best Hiking Season: July-September

Accommodation options include wilderness huts, tent camping, and occasional mountain lodges.

Survival Tips for the Nordkalottleden

■ Bring a Satellite Device: Most of the path has no phone coverage, so bring an emergency GPS or Garmin InReach.

■ Be Bear and Reindeer Aware: Store food correctly and respect wild creatures.

■ Be prepared for river crossings, since several portions lack bridges and require fording rivers.

5.3 The Jotunheimen Traverse, The Ultimate Norwegian Challenge

Jotunheimen—the "Home of the Giants"—is Norway's most fabled mountain range, including Scandinavia's tallest peaks. The Jotunheimen Traverse is a strenuous multi-day walk that takes hikers deep into the heart of this rough, spectacular region, providing some of the greatest alpine trekking in the nation.

I recall ascending Besseggen Ridge, one of the most well-known sections of this route, and admiring the deep blue Gjende Lake on one side and the turquoise Bessvatnet Lake on the other. It seemed like I was traveling down the spine of a sleeping giant.

Why should you hike the Jotunheimen Traverse?

■ Climb Norway's Highest Peaks - The path offers choices for Galdhøpiggen (2,469m) and Glittertind (2,465m).

■ Hut-to-Hut Trekking: Stay in authentic mountain cottages with hot meals and comfy mattresses.

■ Stunning Alpine scenery: snow-capped peaks, glacial lakes, and deep valleys at every turn.

Trail Details:

- Distance: 70-100 kilometers (according to route modifications)
- Time required: 5–7 days
- Difficulty: Hard (steep ascents, variable weather)
- Best Hiking Season: July-September

Accommodation: DNT cabins; wild camping permitted.

Professional Tips for the Jotunheimen Traverse

■ Book Huts in Advance - During high season, DNT cabins fill up quickly, so book early!

■ Be Prepared for Snow, Even in Summer - Higher altitudes may have snowfields year-round.

■ Use Trekking Poles - The steep descents may be difficult on the knees, and poles can help significantly.

Norway's long-distance treks provide something for everyone, from the historic charm of the King's Road to the sheer seclusion of the Nordkalottleden and the rough alpine splendor of Jotunheimen.

If you've never done multi-day hiking before, begin with The King's Trail or a shorter hut-to-hut trip in Jotunheimen. If you're an experienced traveler looking for excitement, the Nordkalottleden Trail can be the perfect challenge.

Whatever path you choose, one thing is certain: you will conclude your journey as a different person than when you began. 🔺🎒

Chapter 6: Seasonal Hiking and Unique Experiences.

Hiking in Norway is more than simply picking a path; it's also about selecting the proper season. Every season changes the terrain, resulting in a unique trip.

Some hikers like the midnight sun, which casts golden light over the sky well after midnight. Others prefer the vibrant hues of autumn when the tundra sparkles in tones of crimson, orange, and gold. Some face the frigid winter landscapes, hiking over snow-covered fjords on snowshoes, while others fantasize about standing on a secluded route, watching the Northern Lights dance above.

In this chapter, we'll look at Norway's most wonderful seasonal experiences, guiding you through the ideal time to walk and what makes each season distinct.

6.1 Midnight Sun Hiking: Trekking Under 24-Hour Daylight

There is something surreal about trekking when the sun never sets. From late May to late July, the summer light shines both day and night in northern Norway, above the Arctic Circle.

I recall my first-midnight sunwalk in Lofoten. It was 2 a.m., yet the sky was filled with warm golden light. A small number of us stood on the peak of Ryten, gazing out over the ocean. We weren't exhausted, but utterly in wonder.

Why Hike Under the Midnight Sun?

■ No time constraint - Hike at any time without regard for sunset.

■ Surreal Lighting: Low-angle sunlight creates lengthy shadows and golden colors throughout the countryside.

■ Cooler Temperatures - Avoid the heat of the day and enjoy a wonderful night time hike.

Best Locations for Midnight Sun Hiking

- The Lofoten Islands include stunning coastal peaks with views of the sea.
- Senja has dramatic cliffs and calm pathways.
- Tromsø and Lyngen Alps provide higher mountains and more demanding treks.
- The northernmost point in mainland Europe is known as Nordkapp (North Cape).

Insider Tips

■ Start in the evening - Many hikers start from 9-10 PM to reach the peak by midnight.

Wear sunglasses since the sun never goes below the horizon and maybe dazzling even late at night.

■ Be Prepared for Cold Air - Even in summer, nighttime temperatures may drop dramatically.

6.2 Winter Hiking and Snowshoe Adventures

Many people believe that trekking ceases in the winter, yet this could not be farther from the truth. Norway's trails change into a winter paradise, with hikes through snow-covered slopes, frozen lakes, and lonely woodlands. Snowshoeing is the finest technique to explore winter paths since it allows you to float over heavy snow without sinking. It's an entirely different kind of journey, and certain paths are even more wonderful in the snow.

I once trekked through Rondane National Park in January, with snowflakes whirling around me and the environment quiet but for the crunch of snow underfoot. It seemed as if I had stepped into another universe, where time had halted and nature had remained intact.

Why Try Winter Hiking?

■ Discover Norway's landscapes in a new light with snow-covered trails.

■ Fewer Crowds, More Solitude - Many popular routes are deserted in winter, providing serene and intimate experiences.

■ Challenging yet rewarding - Snowshoeing provides fantastic exercise and helps develop winter hiking abilities.

Best places for winter hiking and snowshoeing

Rondane National Park has gentle slopes and icy lakes.

- Jotunheimen National Park - More difficult, with alpine scenery.
- Hardangervidda, Norway's biggest alpine plateau, is ideal for multi-day winter hikes.
- Lofoten and Senja are coastal mountains that remain snow-covered long into April.

Winter Hiking Safety Tips:

■ Layer your clothing: base layer (wool), insulation (down or fleece), and waterproof shell.

■ Check Avalanche Conditions: Some regions are prone to avalanches, so always check reports before setting out.

■ Bring a headlamp since sunlight is limited throughout the winter months.

6.3 Top Fall Foliage Hikes in Norway

There is nothing quite like fall in Norway. By mid-September, the mountains had transformed into a sea of red, orange, and gold, with colorful mosses and flaming birch trees dotting the landscape.

What is the best part? Autumn also brings fewer visitors, milder hiking temps, and fewer mosquitoes. If you like fresh air, vibrant colors, and tranquil pathways, now is the time to go trekking.

Standing atop Besseggen Ridge in late September, I recall seeing the valley below shine with golden trees and the highest peaks covered in the first sprinkling of snow. It was one of the most breathtaking vistas I had ever seen.

Why Hike in the Autumn?

■ Incredible Colors - Norway's tundra sparkles in red, orange, and yellow.

■ Fewer Tourists - Quieter trails provide a more serene experience.

■ Cooler Hiking Weather - No more summer heat, simply ideal hiking conditions.

Best Fall Foliage Hikes.

🥾 Besseggen Ridge has bright hues and snow-capped peaks in the distance.

🥾 Rondane National Park, Norway's oldest national park, has magnificent fall colors.

🥾 Dovrefjell: Explore the golden tundra and see wild musk oxen.

🥾 Hardangervidda: Rolling hills filled with fall hues, with fewer tourists.

Insider Tips for Autumn Hiking

■ Go Early in the Season - By mid-October, snow may cover the paths.

■ Prepare for Unpredictable Weather: Bring rain gear and warm layers as fall weather may change quickly.

■ Check Daylight Hours: As the sun sets sooner in the fall, start treks earlier in the day.

6.4 Seeing the Northern Lights on the Trail.

Hiking beneath the Northern Lights is one of the most wonderful experiences in Norway. Imagine standing on a secluded route, surrounded by snow-covered mountains, watching the sky burst in green and purple light waves.

I walked up a little hill near Tromsø late at night, expecting to see the aurora. Just as I was ready to give up, the sky came alive. It was like witnessing a quiet fireworks display, but utterly natural—and amazing.

Where to Hike for the Best Northern Lights Views

- Tromsø is one of Norway's greatest aurora locations.
- Senja - Fewer people and lovely seaside scenery.
- Lofoten Islands - Dramatic landscape with stunning light reflections on fjords.

- Alta and Finnmark have some of Norway's darkest skies, which is ideal for seeing the Northern Lights.

Tips for Aurora Hiking

■ Visit between September and March - The aurora is only visible in the darkest months.

■ Check the Forecast: Use an app like My Aurora Forecast to forecast activity.

■ Bring additional clothing to stay warm while watching the lights!

In Norway, each season has its distinct character. Whether you're hiking beneath the midnight sun, traveling through beautiful autumn landscapes, exploring icy winter paths, or chasing the Northern Lights, you'll see a side of Norway that few others do.

What is the best part? No matter when you arrive, Norway always has something special to offer you.

🌿❄🔥■

Chapter 7: Practical Information for Hikers.

So, you've decided on your ideal walk-in in Norway. Perhaps you're picturing Trolltunga's majestic vistas, the craggy peaks of Lofoten, or a multi-day journey through Jotunheimen. Now comes the actual question: how do you get there? Where are you staying? And how can you ensure everything runs smoothly?

This chapter includes all you need to know regarding transportation, lodging, and family-friendly hiking, allowing you to concentrate on the trip rather than rushing for last-minute arrangements.

7.1 Getting to Trailheads: Transportation and Logistics

One of the most difficult tasks for hikers in Norway is getting to the trailhead. Some popular walks are easily accessible, while others need a combination of boats, buses, and lengthy drives across inaccessible regions.

Let's look at the finest transit alternatives, how much they cost, and which ones are suitable for various climbs.

Public Transportation: Buses, Trains, and Ferries

Norway has a well-developed public transportation system, however, it is not always convenient to get to trailheads. Some treks need numerous transfers or seasonal transportation alternatives.

🚌 Buses: Although dependable, Norway's bus system has limitations in rural regions. Some trails have seasonal shuttle buses.

- The Trolltunga Shuttle Bus (June-September) costs NOK 250-500 round fare from Odda to the higher trailhead.
- Preikestolen Bus (April-October): NOK 200–400 from Stavanger to the trailhead.
- Romsdalseggen Shuttle Bus (June-September) costs NOK 250-350 from Åndalsnes.

🚆 Trains: The Norwegian State Railways (Vy) runs beautiful rail lines, however, most treks need a bus or vehicle from the station.

- Oslo to Bergen Railway (ideal for Hardangervidda hiking): NOK 1,000-1,800 (6-7 hours).
- Trondheim to Bodø Railway (ideal for Lofoten hiking): NOK 900-1,500 (10 hours).

- Ferries: Some fjordside walks need ferry crossings.
  - Geiranger Ferry: NOK 450-600 for hikers going to Skageflå.
  - Moskenes Ferry (Bodø - Lofoten): NOK 250-500, ideal for reaching Lofoten hiking.
  - Renting a car is the best way to reach remote trails.

If you intend on trekking in many regions, hiring a vehicle is the best alternative. Many of Norway's greatest walks are remote, and having a vehicle allows you to explore at your speed.

- Cost breakdown (estimate):
  - Rental car: NOK 800-1,500 per day (cheaper if booked early).
  - Gasoline costs NOK 20-25 per liter.
  - Toll roads: Most highways charge automated tolls (NOK 20-80 per toll station).
  - Ferries with cars cost NOK 100-400, depending on the route.

Guided tours are a hassle-free option.

For those who do not wish to organize their transportation, guided hiking trips include everything—transportation, lodging, and skilled guides.

Trolltunga Guided Hike costs NOK 1,500-2,500 (including transportation from Odda).

Jotunheimen Trek (multi-day): NOK 8,000-15,000 (includes transportation, meals, and hut accommodations).

Northern Lights and Hiking in Senja: NOK 12,000 or more (includes transportation, meals, and guides).

7.2 Where to Stay: Cabins, Camping, and Hotels.

Norway offers a variety of lodging alternatives, including charming mountain cabins, luxurious hotels, and tents beneath the stars.

♣ Norwegian Trekking Association (DNT) Cabins

Norway's DNT huts are the finest alternative for hikers searching for inexpensive and picturesque overnight lodgings. These mountain lodges, self-service cottages, and unstaffed cabins are found throughout Norway's backcountry.

Types of DNT Huts:

- Staffed Lodges: Full-service mountain hotels with meals, beds, and hot showers (NOK 1,000-1,800 each night).
- Self-service huts are basic cottages equipped with a kitchen, bunk beds, and firewood (NOK 350-600 per night).
- Unstaffed Huts: More isolated and often need DNT key access (NOK 250-500 each night).

The best DNT huts for hikers:

- Trolltunga: Skjeggedal Cabin - Near the trailhead.
- Jotunheimen: Gjendebu - Beautiful place near Lake Gjende.
- Hardangervidda: Haukeliseter Fjellstue - An excellent base for winter trekking.

▲ Camping: A Budget-Friendly Adventure Option

Norway's Right to Roam statute (Allemannsretten) allows you to camp nearly anywhere in nature—for free!

Camping tips:
■ Stay at least 150 meters away from private dwellings.
■ Use existing campsites in vulnerable areas.
■ Pack thick sleeping bags (even summer evenings might be chilly).

⬢ Where Not to Camp:
- ⊘ National parks have limits (see local regulations).
- ⊘ Private farmland without authorization.
- 💰 Paid campsites cost NOK 200-500 per night and include showers, toilets, and grilling facilities.

🏠 Hotels and guesthouses.
For hikers who want more comfort, Norway provides hotels and guesthouses in most towns along major hiking trails.

💰 Average price per night:
- Budget Hotels and Hostels: NOK 600–1,200.
- Mid-Range Hotels: NOK 1,500–2,500
- Luxury Hotels & Lodges: NOK 3000+

7.3 Hiking with Kids and Families

Hiking in Norway is not only for hard-core explorers; it's also a fantastic experience for families. Many paths are kid-friendly, and Norwegian culture promotes outdoor activities from a young age.

Best family-friendly hikes
● Easy walks:
- Preikestolen (Pulpit Rock) - Moderate, but manageable for energetic children (8+ years).
- Husedalen Valley - A gentle valley trek with waterfalls.
- Brevandring Jostedalsbreen offers guided glacier hikes (for children aged 6 and above).

▲ Fun multi-day hikes for families:
- Dovrefjell Musk Ox Safari - Follow simple routes to see wild musk oxen.
- Hardangervidda Cabin-to-Cabin walks are short daily walks between DNT cabins.
- Lofoten's Beach Camping Hikes - Easy treks lead to white sand beaches.

Tips For Hiking With Kids

■ Choose shorter hikes (3-5 km) with enjoyable stops along the way.

■ Bring extra snacks for kids to improve their energy levels.

■ Let Kids Lead - Provide a little map and encourage exploring.

■ Prepare for unpredictable weather by packing additional clothing and raincoats.

Planning a trek in Norway requires some work, but the payoff is breathtaking natural beauty. Whether you're exploring distant trails, staying in charming cottages, or introducing your children to hiking for the first time, Norway offers an experience for you. So go out there, explore the trails, and experience Norway's raw beauty!

▲

Chapter 8: Local Culture and Hiking Stories

Hiking in Norway is about more than simply following trails through stunning scenery; it's about immersing yourself in the country's rich cultural legacy, with each mountain, valley, and fjord telling a tale. Whether it's old troll folktales or the rich customs of the indigenous Sámi people, hiking here ties you to millennia of storytelling and history.

8.1 Norwegian Folktales and Legends Regarding Mountains

Norway's mountains and fjords are more than simply picturesque; they're also full of tales and traditions handed down through centuries. If you've ever glanced at a craggy peak and felt it was almost too dramatic to be true, Norwegian legend says you're not wrong. Many of these mountains were once giants and trolls, but the rising sun turned them into stone.

Trolltunga (The Troll's Tongue)

One of Norway's most renowned treks, Trolltunga (The Troll's Tongue), is more than simply a dangerous rock ledge; it's a frozen moment in a troll's existence. According to legend, a troll once stood here, insulting the gods with his spread tongue. But when morning came over the fjords, the troll was taken off guard. The sun turns him into stone, and he sits there, constantly pointing his tongue out over the valley.

Hiker's Tip: If you trek Trolltunga on a foggy morning, with clouds whirling over the cliffs, you may see why people believed in such things.

Jotunheimen: The Land of Giants.

Jotunheimen, Norway's tallest mountain range, translates as "Home of the Jotnar"—the Norse mythological giants. These mountains were thought to be governed by massive creatures of incredible power. Even Odin, the All-Father of the Norse gods, dreaded the Jotnar and their might.

The peaks of Jotunheimen, such as Galdhøpiggen and Glittertind, were thought to be giants' strongholds, with their residences concealed deep beneath the valleys. Some people still believe that if you trek here alone, particularly at twilight, you may hear distant echoes of the Jotnar's footsteps across the mountains.

Hiker's Tip: If you spend the night in a DNT cabin deep in Jotunheimen, go outside and listen—the quiet is almost otherworldly.

Nøkken, the Water Spirit of the Fjords.

Not all of Norway's myths include mountains. The Nøkken, a mysterious water ghost who lures visitors to their demise, may be found deep beneath the fjords and lakes. Folklore describes the Nøkken as a lovely horse waiting at the water's side, beckoning tired trekkers to ride it. However, once a person climbs, the Nøkken gallops into the lake, pulling them into the depths forever.

Some hikers in Norway's isolated areas claim to have witnessed odd ripples in calm water, even when there's no breeze, indicating the Nøkken is watching.

Hiker's Tip: If you're trekking near fjords or lakes, you'll often notice little waterfalls cascading down the rocks. Norwegians refer to this as "Huldredråper"—the tears of the mythological woodland spirit Hulder, who also figures in folktales.

8.2 Cultural Hiking Experience with the Sámi People.

Hiking in Northern Norway takes you into the lands of the Sámi, Scandinavia's indigenous people. The Sámi have been living in Norway's Arctic for thousands of years, following reindeer migratory paths, coexisting with nature, and retaining one of Europe's oldest civilizations.

Hiking in Finnmark, Troms, or Nordland takes you through landscapes that Sámi ancestors have frequented for ages. If you look closely, you may see remnants of their culture that are still there today.

Learning about Sámi culture on the trail.

Many hiking trails pass through old Sámi territories, where you may still observe traditional communities known as "siida"—groups of families who herd reindeer together. If you're fortunate, you could see a Sámi herder herding his reindeer across the highlands.

Here are several methods to explore Sámi culture while hiking:

- Hike in Karasjok or Kautokeino, the core of Sámi culture in Norway.
- Visit Sámi lavvu (traditional tent) - Some guided treks include stops at Sámi camps to hear tales from locals.
- Experience traditional Sámi cuisine in Tromsø or Alta, including Bidos (reindeer stew) and smoked salmon.

The Northern Lights and Sámi Mythology

If you go trekking in the fall or winter, you may see one of Norway's most spectacular natural wonders: the Aurora Borealis. For the Sámi, the Northern Lights were sacrosanct.

According to Sámi folklore, the lights represent the ghosts of the dead dancing across the sky. People were told in ancient times not to whistle at the Northern Lights because doing so may draw them down to earth and bring ill luck.

If you hike in Tromsø, Lofoten, or Senja between September and March, you have a high possibility of witnessing the lights. Find a dark, open spot away from city lights and gaze up; you can see the ghosts dancing.

Hiking in Norway is more than simply breathtaking scenery; it's also about trekking through live history and folklore. Every mountain, fjord, and valley has a story, and hiking here allows you to become a part of it.

Whether you're following the footsteps of trolls, hiking in the land of giants, or visiting the Sámi, Norway's trails provide more than simply an environment; they link you to a rich and wonderful history.

So the next time you step foot on a Norwegian path, take a minute to listen. Who knows. Maybe the mountains are still whispering their ancient tales.

Chapter 9: Final Tips and Resources.

Every wonderful experience deserves a well-planned conclusion. You should now be prepared to explore Norway's magnificent routes, from iconic peaks to hidden jewels. But, before you lace on your boots and go out, here are a few last-minute must-haves to help you navigate, remain safe, and make the most of your Norwegian hiking adventure.

9.1 Recommended Hiking Apps and Websites

Even in a nation as wild as Norway, technology can be a great hiking companion. Whether you want downloadable maps, real-time weather updates, or thorough route descriptions, these applications and websites will be very useful.

Best Apps for Hikers in Norway.

📍 **Norwegian Trekking Association (UT.no)**
- The preferred app for accurate trail maps, hiking routes, and cabin locations.
- It offers trail difficulty ratings, seasonal guidance, and GPX files for navigation.
- An offline option is available—ideal for distant treks!
- Download at https://www.ut.no/.

📕 **Norwegian Kart Outdoors**
- Norway's finest precise topographic maps are essential for wilderness trekkers.
- Shows elevation, pathways, and national park borders.
- Works offline using pre-downloaded maps.
- Download at https://www.kartverket.no/.

⛺ **Norwegian Meteorological Institute's Weather App (YR.no)**
- Extremely precise weather predictions for mountain areas.
- Hourly reports on wind, rain, and temperature are critical for planning safe trips.
- Download at https://www.yr.no/.

📡 FatMap
- A 3D map tool that is ideal for analyzing geography, elevation, and path steepness.
- Ideal for planning routes in hilly locations.
- Premium users may access this functionality offline.
- Download at https://www.fatmap.com/.

🎒 *Don't book hotels.*
- This software allows you to simply reserve Norwegian Trekking Association (DNT) lodges.
- Displays real-time availability of mountain chalets.
- Download at https://hyttebooking.dnt.no/.
- 📡 Hjelp 113, the Norwegian Emergency App.
- Send your GPS coordinates immediately to emergency personnel.
- Provides direct call alternatives for Norwegian rescue services.
- Download at https://www.113.no/.

9.2 Emergency Contacts and Resources.

Even the best-prepared hikers sometimes encounter unforeseen problems. If you ever become lost, wounded, or in need of assistance, here's who to contact and what to do.

Norwegian Emergency Numbers:
- 📞 110, Fire & Rescue
- 📞 112, Police
- 📞 113, Medical Emergencies

Norwegian Mountain Rescue Service
- Norwegian Red Cross Rescuers (Røde Kors Hjelpekorps) are trained volunteers who help in mountain rescues.
- The Norwegian Alpine Rescue Group (NARG) consists of specialized teams that work in harsh situations.

If you are in a rural place with no mobile service, consider going to higher ground for better reception. If there is no signal, locate a safe place and wait for other hikers to pass—Norwegians are highly kind and will aid if necessary.

9.3 Maps

Having a good map might be the difference between a pleasant trek and an unexpected overnight stay in the mountains. Here are some of the most useful printable maps for Norwegian hiking trails:

📌 **Official Norwegian maps.**
Norwegian Mapping Authority (Kartverket) provides free topographic maps of Norway.
- Visit https://www.kartverket.no/Kart/Norgeskart.
- UT.no Trail Maps are ideal for organizing walks and discovering DNT cottages.
- Visit https://www.ut.no/kart/.

🔖 Norwegian Trekking Association (DNT) paper maps, available at bookshops and tourist centers. Visit https://www.dntbutikken.no/.

🔖 OpenStreetMap Hiking Norway offers free, community-sourced hiking paths.
🔗 https://www.openstreetmap.org.

You're now completely prepared to tackle Norway's stunning hiking routes, whether you're climbing Trolltunga, exploring Jotunheimen, or chasing the Northern Lights in Tromso.

Your Final To-Do List Before Hitting the Trail:

- Download your maps and applications.
- Check the weather forecast.
- Inform someone about your trekking plan.
- Pack the appropriate gear.
- Respect nature and leave no trace.

Norway's paths await you. It's time to lace up, walk outside, and let the adventure begin! 🚶 ⛰

Made in the USA
Thornton, CO
04/23/25 21:54:13

563372ff-e803-4020-a003-97bef0db397cR01